T0166327

A LIGHTNESS, A THIRST, OR NOTHING AT ALL

ALSO BY ADELE KENNY

Poetry
What Matters
The Kite & Other Poems from Childhood
Chosen Ghosts
At the Edge of the Woods
Starship Earth
Castles and Dragons
Questi Momenti
Migrating Geese
Between Hail Marys
Illegal Entries
The Roses Open
An Archaeology of Ruins
Notes from the Nursing Home

Nonfiction
Chapbooks: A Historical Perspective
Staffordshire Figures: History in Earthenware 1740–1900
Photographic Cases: Victorian Design Sources 1840–1870
Staffordshire Animals: A Collector's Guide
Staffordshire Spaniels: A Collector's Guide
We Become By Being
The Silence and the Flame: Clare and Francis of Assisi
Counseling Gifted, Creative, and Talented Youth Through the Arts
A Creative Writing Companion

A LIGHTNESS, A THIRST, OR NOTHING AT ALL

Adele Kenny

Welcome Rain Publishers
NEW YORK

Welcome Rain Publishers
217 Thompson Street, #473
New York, New York 10012

www.welcomerain.com

ISBN-13: 978-1566493963
ISBN-10: 156649396X

Library of Congress Cataloging Data is available.

Book design by Smythtype Design

For Charles DeFanti
and
Chaucer Kenny

Every one of us is shadowed by an illusory person:
a false self.
We are not very good at recognizing illusions,
least of all the ones we cherish about ourselves.

Our reality, our true self, is hidden in what appears to us
to be nothingness . . .

—Thomas Merton, *New Seeds of Contemplation*

CONTENTS

PART III — THIS

PART I

✦

ALL THINGS CONSIDERED

What She Means

Even if the asters were permanent, the last crickets under the pine still fully alive, fully present—the balance not so easily tipped. Even had she kept what she couldn't, it was always this: what stayed broken—literal dust and the way light thinned.

She thinks of the house in the mountains, how rain settled for days in the hollow between two hills—without thunder, without stopping—the way rain sounded then, the field's dim glistening. She remembers how wet earth pushed its cold up, the creek overfilled, fast over fallen leaves, the leaves singing— how it feels (that wanting to go home)—the mortal act of are and are not. That simple, that clear.

Now it's about what lasts, the way nothing ends without pouring itself out—chrysanthemums shattered by rain, light that lingers in lessening light—what she means when she says *my life is not this* or that she is not really here.

Always That Thought

Always that thought when you least expect it—the one your life trips on—when the sky falls, one blue grain at a time, and you tumble the way Alice did through the hole.

If you think about it, you know the triggers: the guilts (of course), your friend's suicide, your mother's long death. Being strong has worn you down: this is your frailty, the part of you that needs the pills, the part that stays inside the shadow.

On days like this, you fall through the world into places between; ghost of this, ghost of that and, no, you've never been who they thought you were.

Something of What

The old house gone and nothing but stars where a rooftop touched the sky; her room lit by candles—one in the window, one by the door. We know something of what happened: the way she tied herself to the world through memory, how she trusted the past, even the wreck and debris of it. Predictable diminuendos.

Tonight it's one part now, four parts déjà vu. A white mouse in the door of her dream looks into the trap when everything, it seems, means something else.

And There

She knows she has risen from the bed, her feet cold on the floor, the room still dark. She walks deeper into what feels like a dream—the length and core of it. Somewhere—far—a night bird bends its wings to the river. She feels herself drift—form without form. High on a cliff, bare trees nudge the sky. She remembers this dream, opens her arms, and (without looking down) moves one foot forward. The sky fills with ghosts and stars. *Regret nothing*, she thinks.

What You Know

A stray dog laps the moon from a broken flowerpot. Silk hydrangeas bloom against the fence. A heron stands on the clothesline—bluer than blue—perched where (sky, earth) edges converge.

On the wall, the painting of a clock ticks, hands painted in at three forty-seven. She takes a wax apple from the bowl and peels it with a silver fruit knife. Sugared bread dries on the table. Across the room, a dimensional window masquerades as persuasion. If you believe it, it is.

What (she says)

There is the piece of wood. There, the stone. Not quite amulets.

One or two might call her crazy. *Why Not?* she asks (white hair tied back with white string). *The question is the same question (everything it is) no matter how you ask it* . . .

Make no mistake—this is only the current failure and what will do (or have to do) for now. Make no mistake, she says (sometimes barefoot, sometimes wearing a single shoe).

Despite Her Attachment

Sometimes she forgets that, despite her attachment to the world, breath and flesh are not enough. Her long-dead, grim and entrenched in their silt and stone, hum softly. So much grief. So much in this detachment—what it means— the collapses, the vanishings. She pushes back the rules of engagement—battles, dramas. Clarity happens—sometimes by accident, sometimes by invitation.

The oak creates its own intensity, and the flowers (their soft hearts deeply rooted). She looks for more than what is in things, and silence that is not indifferent.

The rain becomes a fine drizzle (the shape and feel of it). A deer and her fawn stand where the meadow bends into forest, their hooves gold-splashed in yellow flowers: the trick is to not want what you don't have.

That Night

The trouble with dreams is this: none is ever exact, what stays with us mostly peripheral—a shadow in the stairwell, what might have been whispers in the hall. False awakenings . . .

That night in England, my window (high in the wall) opened over a churchyard. It was autumn, a subtle change in the sun, the air a little thinner. Even the crickets (strained voices like far-off rain) had lost their grip on the light. Mysteries unique to October . . .

I'm still not sure what I saw or didn't see, how much was in the dream (or something more): the child's sunken stone (a small, granite lamb that leaned into earth), the church's lesser door (open). And then, a long line of my dead, their faces turned away; above them, a kestrel, brief on the clouds' surface—there and then not. Only the stones . . .

Dry leaves rattled against the graves. My candle sputtered (struck matches beside it)—mist in the distance; and sheep, separate and silent, on the hill . . .

The Silence After

Late December: afternoon deepens and retreats, shadows fall on rows of stones. A broken column tilts at the sky. There is snow in the air, pale leaves under ice.

Across the river, a woodpecker taps into its own sound. Here, where trees edge darkly toward water, we measure our shadows' exactness. Deep in that absent light, chapel bells ring the hour.

Whatever we came for isn't here, only *remember* or *wish*, if we think in those terms—and nothing to keep us (no token, no resemblance of things), nothing to carry home.

No One Said

It wasn't always like this. No one said *stop* or *listen*. No words for *waste* and *break*—no words like bright birds, the names of things—only the burned trees, the snapped connection. Even the air was fictional—the moon absent-eyed, the water cloud-ridden—whole nights shot through by men on their way to redemption. (One man had nothing to lose and the girl took it from him. Another man took the girl.) But now, arpeggioed stars (triggered and carved) are a shifting remix of dark and light. In theoretical physics, black holes and stargates are real. Between her and the sky, someone slams a door.

Nothing Specific

Our moon floats away from the earth, an inch and a half each year—an inch and a half (already centuries in process)—and no sound on the moon's surface (the depth of that stillness, that silent floating). What we say matters, and how we touch.

The moon will disappear; like all bodies, it will lose definition, craters and shape; it will pull back its last tide as if it had never been (one last wave, the wind behind it)—and one day the sun will explode into space like a broken smoke ring, one glorious puff. Nothing specific to prove what was or is—no small because.

Oh, Leonardo

Soldiers and priests in the dark arcade. Your final note written backwards. Under a pale-milk sky, cowbells ring in the distance. I knew I'd never find you there, not past the fallen farms and leaning fences. Nothing changes the reality of things.

Under pitched windows, a strung voice climbs the ivy— abject, strangely changed, of no interest now in this doubtful light. And what did loneliness mean except that it was almost winter—our last conversation remembered back into words. What I imagine is memory may only be something I dream.

The flower lady, I see, still sells flowers—bunches of poppies, blue delphiniums—her basket over-brimmed, almost flowing. All down the street, she crosses and re-crosses her shadow, every stone cobbled (like old shoes and worship). I would have met you there in Covent Garden (some diva wailing Puccini inside the opera house, a street performer juggling knives), and you would have said, *Go ahead, dance*. But what am I thinking? I'd be alone, you gone back to Florence or France.

A cabbage moth flutters up, out of my own shadow, ephemeral, a scrap of paper. Time and tenses are fixed in this moment— nothing moves (as if this were permanent). I think *almost*. I haven't forgotten the pact we made. I kept my promise, and then you were dead. What never happened will never change.

Lately, I have this sense of nothing that makes sense; and these regrets, like all regrets, have come too late. I have no idea what I would do differently, what old hope we felt, or what the one thing was that neither of us could name. The dark is convincing but, oh, Leonardo, it's morning somewhere and maybe, just maybe . . .

All Things Considered

Night on both sides of the day—steep in reliefs and bereavements. Like autumn's cuff, still brilliant but frayed, she settles for change (the advantages of limitation)—a nuthatch at the feeder. Between clouds and configured dreams, she looks back with surprising closeness, and loves and loves without knowing why—anything beautiful, everything brief.

PART II

✦

WHATEVER MEANING

. . . in this loneliness

I have no idea what year it was, but long ago when Joe (who
ground tools on the night shift) called in sick and showed up
early with a half-cooked ham that we sliced and fried. There
were seven or eight of us, maybe ten: Deborah, Alex, Charlie
and Charlie's wife (who brought a basket of oranges). After
we ate, we talked and sat until nearly dawn; there was wine,
of course, and beer—we drank, we smoked. Someone read a
poem by Rod McKuen, and we all booed, then one of us (was
it Deborah?) read André Breton's "Always for the First Time."
We closed our eyes and nodded (the memory says in unison,
but probably not).

Joe played his guitar and sang about grief and, because he
made it up as he went along, it sounded like an Irish lament,
so some of us cried until Edie began to sing about porpoises
and orifices—every off rhyme that night a holy thing in the
shifting distance between songs: something Charlie said about
ice, something Joe said about God. That night, Joe discovered
a spire of moonlight inside my pine tree, professed and praised
between boughs. And one star's white suddenness stunned us
all the way a pearl disorients the eye.

I think of Edie (God-knows-where in Pennsylvania) and Charlie
dead—things we did (and almost did), the shook sidewalk of
when, what we call *was*, what we thought we knew—so close to
listening—the ladders we built to stand under (and fell from).

Schweitzer said, *We are all so much together, but we are all dying
of loneliness.* (That's how it was with us.) Merton said, . . . *it is in
this loneliness that the deepest activities begin.* And so it began—
us at the curb waving each other home—waving, praying for
what we were, what we might become—and loneliness still our
best defense.

Even Now

Memory is easy here, in springtime's rimless light—only a little rain to pattern the sky. There's a faint (perhaps remembered) scent of meadow grass and wild thyme. Something sweet that stays where shadows gather.

For nearly forty years, your death has been a grief that only now begins to know its name. All this time, I've rebuilt you out of dead leaves and wind, dumb with a feeling that even now, I can't express—as if that dark were your happiness and you ran to it, years too young to be dead—as if, even now, you might open your hand and reach through time to where I wait.

Something Like Icarus

Imagine Icarus before the air let go / before the sea lunged up. Imagine the / downward pitch, the boy wing-tipped / and sticky. / Of course he failed, we all / fail.

And what moves now in the attic bedroom, the cellar three floors down? What step in the hallway above? How much stays as we left it in this old house where night still climbs the front stairs, and something inside tries to shine?

I walk through rooms smaller than memory made them (the old clock on its shelf—rows of books, their titles still warm). Upstairs, a child stands at her bedroom window. I know this child. Any sound in the dark, and she was afraid—even before she learned what changes things.

In this old town with its brown river and empty places, dusk raises the wind. No one here remembers who we were or how we left. The little girl turns her head and whispers: *Daddy, I came so close . . .*

Halloween

Trick-or-treaters come to the door repeatedly—little ones
early, older kids into the night until she runs out of candy and
turns off the outside lights. The wall between worlds is thin
(aura over aura—stars flicker and flinch). The woman buttons
her coat, checks her reflection in the mirror, and stands cheek
to glass (eye on her own eye, its abstract edge). She leaves the
house (empty house that we all become)—shadows shaped to
the trees, crows in the high branches.

Why Blueberries?

And why now, years after, do I suddenly think of you, the way darkness remembers light? This morning even the shadows are warm, the berries sweet, and I think of that one afternoon (our lips stained, fingertips blue). It was all you and then—all feeling. The whole world floated over us—almost touchable— as we lay in the grass and ate blueberries. Like most young loves, we ended sadly. What I remember is what lingered: a shining, silvery thing; the warbler that day, flight in its song. I think of you the way the living remember the dead—more than they were—a kind of loving.

In That Instant

Just there . . . in a lapse that time shifts through . . . I remember my yellow scarf, your gold earring, the way clouds dragged their shadows into the river—sky and water. (Blue. White. Gray.) That day we climbed the side of a covered bridge, onto the roof—the pitch hard-angled, dangerously steep. Narrow planks lifted and dipped where we stepped—so easy to be that reckless, that young. When you pulled me close at the top and kissed me, someone below yelled *jump*. In that instant, I almost thought we might.

That Should Have Been

Insistent the distant rain, and what between us? Was it that morning (the blue of that morning), the symmetry of left and right—one, two, one, two? Or dead leaves—the way they clung to our shoes and walked with us over the patched gravel? No, and no—nor was it the sky (thunder-colored), the tulip tree beating with wings (me lost in my own absence). It wasn't the way night fell in empty rooms, the way air moved in the space behind you—all the small givens. I said you were right, that should have been enough.

Whatever Meaning

Sometimes it's easy to lose your place—you forget where you are—and the language (no matter how precise or lush) promises nothing. Allotments thin, shadows on one side of the wall repeat on the other. You know that something important is missing—its possibility felt. Imagine the feeling: as if your foot just missed a stair (trip and fall), the enchantment, not just passing, already gone (the bell-rope short—a tragedy of what we imagined). Rough-meshed or meticulous, it's an unpredictable edge. Whatever meaning we give it later, we weren't made to be safe.

Once Upon a . . .

Lost in the woods, they feel (as much as see) the way trees darken before the sky. In faded light, they crawl through weeds (poisonous sumac, false strawberry). Lichen and moss stick to their knees. They are not Hansel and Gretel, not brother and sister. They don't know about witches or metaphor (which, of course, this is), but they understand that the air is colder than it was when they entered the forest. Darkness wells around them and creates new shadows. They feel the prickle of briars and stars—splinter and hiss in the underbrush—something goat-footed behind them. Cold, pale—their lips taste like moonlight. When the witch appears, they will follow her. They will live in the cage. They will eat gingerbread and grow fat. They will both be angry and sad.

Not in the Words

Not the wind that muffles her view, not the dirt road. Not light drawn into the trees, or the forest she made to lose herself in. Not the house or the people who slipped through. Not the gun in her night table drawer (its mother-of-pearl handles) or the moon or a dog that barks across the street. Not the long, awkward pauses; not the quiet like ruins. Only what, finally, has no cost.

As Easy As

I remember *downpour* and *torrent*: wildflowers hammered and bent, everything drenched—a stitch in my side from running. Rain on the path ankle-deep over broken stones, and rising. When I stopped (pine and sage in the air—three thousand miles from home), you appeared the way an idea slips into consciousness, at first on my vision's edge and then suddenly— the moon haloed, raindrops pearled with flickering light. And there we were—rich in our skin. As easy as that. As basic as need.

The Man on the Train

The man in the seat next to me leans out of his into mine and says, *I'm a pathological loser.* Two wives left him for other men, one for a soldier of fortune, the current wife is having an affair (at least, that's what he believes). *Look at me, I'm a ghost,* he whispers, *another pointless addendum.* (Across the aisle, a woman mutters to no one in particular.) I shrug my shoulders. I don't usually ride this train. *Next time,* he says, *I'll get it right,* then mumbles, *more or less.* His eyes are zeroes. What do you say to a man like that?

Better Remembered

She didn't figure on details (a leak in the roof and what it would cost to fix), just this sun and this warmth; not a linear narrative—one-dimensional like the first word she ever spoke then repeated again and again until she was sure what it meant.

Once, time slowed for summer, the trees agreed on shade—but it's all become unlikely, better remembered than it was. This time, she's not concerned with what's certain. The oak tree fills a bigger length of sky, the maple ages. There's a story on the shelf, just within reach, and she wants to change it.

So Much Life

The girl who killed herself, her dog, and son speaks to me.
She tells me that *this* death is only sleep. I'm not sure what she
means by *this*—what *other* death? I stand above her grave, not
knowing if there even is a grave (a place to put her—perhaps
just ash, the newspapers didn't say); but, no, I see her face. Her
lips move before the words: *So much life*, she says, *is dead before
the body follows*. She looks at me through stippled eyes and,
reaching up, she trims the moon with pinking shears. Light,
unraveled, falls (a perfect circle) around the dog beside her—
the dog's spirit scratches its jaw. I don't know how she came
to be inside my dream or why she haunts me—I barely knew
her. From my front porch, I see the house in which she lived—
the storm door open. Snow that is ice, that is glass, covers the
lawn; the lawn splinters and cracks.

Just Perhaps

(After *Ophelia* by John Everett Millais)

Buoyed by her dress, she barely breaks the water's surface—
arms outstretched, palms upturned. Pansies float above her
skirt. There are daisies on the glassy stream, and, there (to
the left, above her head), a bird on the pollard from which she
jumped or fell. Broken willow, broken bough.

And just perhaps, as Hamlet's mother said, she's still alive
and singing—see, her mouth is open, and her eyes; and just
perhaps, she doesn't know how close to death she is—or why
this painting makes me think of you. *Your* death was not
offstage the way Ophelia's was (the ladder placed, the rope
around your neck); nor was the way you parted from yourself,
the silent swinging—only air beneath your feet.

If It Hadn't Been

We wouldn't be here if it hadn't been for the rain, the wind-loosened trees (this quiet shelter); and I wouldn't tell you how nothing wonderful ever matches its memory, how not going home is a sadness we all carry. I wouldn't tell you what I know about losing, how what we keep is never all that we need.

How She Grieved

What can I tell you about the woman with the aqua hat, the woman with six birds, a parrot on her shoulder—the wall she cut through to build a room for the birds, and how, years later, they died—even the parrot, even the one blue finch—how she grieved for their wings, for what she learned from their cages and songs. If you listen, you will hear her call them back, their absence and presence the same.

If, on Christmas Eve

No more than a handful of stars, an ancient chill and something in it like the way we dream before we know we're asleep. The whole idea that this is important—untimed, serious.

Here, where day turns its back, your headlights bring the forest close. Tamaracks blend and blur with oaks, deeper into a night that is tall and dark. O, *Holy* Night. No birds to sing or give thanks. No flash of wings, no glittering incidentals.

The road thins to a line between two sides of the forest—all the green walls lean inward (where you might have entered)—a steeple distant, above. For a moment, the sky takes you with it—one brief, immaculate moment (one small Bethlehem). Somewhere, it's midnight inside a church—the lights just coming on.

as if (this)spring

(After E. E. Cummings)

the rooms you left will forget you, that is, there (where you were, alive only) but now this delicateyellow—prim-and-rose—and (ah) green—peeper and leaf.

your hands stretch first beyond the porch, beyond the hands of your hands—first to feel the rain, which is violet, which is iris, which is not dead—and all this wished for—(as if) crows cleared from your eyes—here, this wing (open) this murmur and melt—(this)spring—(this) something(more) and nothing broken.

What to Expect of Heaven

At least some sense of matter and rust—eyes that remember who you were, hands that know how light feels—the old house, there, in a space between clouds (your father on the porch and your mother)—your dogs (all of them)—larkspur and birds (the plain brown ones, the cardinals)—a place to sit and listen in on those who are still alive, to remember what living was like—a place to dream of breathing.

When the Angel

Nothing at the window, nothing in the sky, but something like hands on your shoulders (a rustle and brush of wings). What you almost don't feel—a voice like leaves inside the trees— barely, almost no sound (imagine a pre-dawn sparrow, its slipped-between song)—cryptic whisper, whisper like cloud. And light! So much light you can't see around it. Imagine that. Imagine the wings behind you, yourself enfolded. Imagine yourself—that safe.

PART III

THIS

Not Just

And so conversion, but not what you think: the floor that turns into a river, the day's last blue before it becomes something deeper. What changes isn't space, or anything remote. The dream dreams itself out of sleep and into the street. The street wanders. Having done what you wanted, you see it was always there (beyond margins and claims), not just the idea of it. What is given, what remains—everything that ends or just begins.

One Day

Have you ever wondered why, in dreams, you're always so alone or why, like leaves over stones, one month tips into another— one day's margins mixed into the next—and you scarcely keep track until one day you can't find the year behind you? Why, when sunset pulls the moon up over your eyes (Shelley's hectic red in the trees), when the sky lapses above rooftops, arches into stars, and you follow the moon's upward march, you want the seclusion that is wonder, that is rest (something you know softly). And you don't have to say *lost* or *misplaced*.

About the Answers

It's only when you're sure there *are* no answers. Nothing absolute—everything between. It's what happens when you stand on a bridge that stars rush under, and you stop asking why (the rain exhausted, the sky a steamed window).

It doesn't matter that you can't identify the weeds by name (or the berries that are poison). High on the blind, white wall a bird calls then falls silent—five runes in your bowl and always something to lose (in the space around you, right where you are). But about the answers, there's no argument: what darkens turns light.

Because Someone Told Me
That Happiness Is an Inside Job

Sooner or later, you get it right—all things that can't be, all things that can't. You stop dreaming out loud and something (whatever it is) tells you to reconcile with what you want and what you choose (what stays still, what moves). You can't insist on happiness, that's not it; but failure doesn't get the last word. Other inventions aside, what you want is one small, infinite space when the truth shifts its weight. And so it is . . . you go there and come back a different person. It happens like that.

Twilight and What There Is

The gauze eyelid is gone and your spun glass hand. The past that always knew where to find you has lost its place. The ghosts have forgotten your name. There's nothing left for the dead to remember—nothing catches up (there's no meter running).

New grass lifts the field—bloodroot, bluebells, a thousand things so small and flawless they almost go unnoticed. Translation doesn't escape you: you're grateful for sunset's watery rust and this, something instinctive called into being, more than perceived. More than memory, more than moment—nothing provisional. Anything you might say, might think, would be too much. You open your palms in a dusky Rorschach and let the dark fall through.

You Reach a Certain Age

And sometimes the weight of it gets to you, this language of leaving, of holding on. It's nothing to do with what gets lifted up—a river holds whatever the sky throws into it, a bird that has no need of earth flies away. You reach a certain age and begin to see how things unwind, the way it all plays out. You learn what's essential, what's not, and it hardly matters what the world was like when you first tried to exalt it. There are rooms in your life unaccounted for, but you can live with that. (Remember the room you slept in as a child? In less time than you spent there, the sun turned its curtains into dust.) You push back your chair and get up. Outside, a neighbor's cat stitches and re-stitches the same torn hem, its yellow eye in line with the moon.

Everything Exactly

What rises up between night and night—the earth deep in moss and peat, the sky herringboned with clouds that float like spindrift. I take nothing for granted: the cicadas rush of song, and the birds (listen, listen). The past in its place, everything present dear and important.

We learn how to live in this later light—far trees stooped at the meadow's edge—everything exactly where it's supposed to be.

Without Seeing

It isn't now or this patch of blue autumn, light skimmed like milk without substance (its ghost on my lips). Or the way trees darken before the sky, the way light slants through pines (my neighbor's lamp or the moon). It's not the way night feels when I walk in March, when snow melts into mud, and I smell grass again; when I know, without seeing, that tight buds open high in the branches. It's not the expected order of things but moments of *other* (when something startles you into knowing *something* other).

Tonight, wind pulled leaves from the sky to my feet and, suddenly (without warning) a deer leapt from the thicket behind me—leapt and disappeared—past me as I passed myself, my body filled with absence, with air, a perfect mold of the light gone through it.

The Way a Soul

Snow rises on a base of ice—twilight all day. Now, the oaks are layered, the pines a ragged wall. The wind takes its work into drifts and fills a squirrel's nest high in the maple (packed leaves over twigs, deeply covered). In this kind of snow, the world loses shape the way a soul loses itself to something greater. The moon slides sideways across the sky, its nimbus thin. My breath's reverse silhouette settles its white against the dark.

No Other World

Chaucer sits on my lap, both of us "sighing from time to time" with Charles Simic's "My Turn to Confess." Chaucer lifts one ear and turns his head from side to side. His tail wags. He likes this poet's voice, so I play the recording again. Sad title, crooked branch. It is winter; it is cold, too late for leaves, only a thin sun over the yard—the old pin oak and the bird in it, the tamarack's shadow in deeper shade. Cloud and wind . . . the furnace hums . . .

Then There Is

Weather patterns change—all patterns change. With this early thaw, winter spools across sidewalks and rivers there. The hydrangeas we trimmed last fall rise like new memories— diffused light where leaves begin—the flip of passage (there, here). A chipmunk under the pines searches ahead of me. It's a pure distinction, what you see (then, now).

Clouds and wind meet in the same direction. I pass myself at the corner, nod, and continue walking—my tracks in the mud behind me.

What You See All Night

The wild bird you catch and let go—what you see all night at
the corner of your eye (along the outline of unfolded wings)—
when the self gives itself up (a bell diffused into air)—more
idea than expression:

a lightness, a thirst, or nothing at all.

We Go from One

We go from one mystery to another: things we said and don't remember (as real as what we don't know); and mysteries like birds that migrate by starlight. I hear them when I walk at night, I see them at the edges of the moon, never quite sure where that movement fits—what freezes or flies, what's free of reason and meaning.

What I counted on has changed. I've learned to expect little, but what some call a deadening isn't: each year there is spring and the peonies, the way they stand their ground in this shaken world, the way we go from one mystery to another only to learn that *we* are the mystery, that the search ends with the searcher—vanisher and vanishing—a particular unknowing.

Even If You Could Explain It Completely

The backstory doesn't matter—this is about what happens now. You open your eyes, move your legs slowly, flex and bend, stretch (aligned to the air). Your puppy looks up at you and wags his tail—he wants to go out. You open the back door and he runs through, happy to sniff the parsley, squat and pee, follow an ant with his nose—the wick of his small body fired with visible joy.

When it happens (really *happens*), it's not complicated. First, what you *really* want—the surprise of it—and then desire. Even if you could explain it completely, you wouldn't. Day becomes day, and night—their passing nothing to do with time. All notion of distance disappears—what feels like entering. Suddenly (like walking into a light you know), you discover this: the certainty that nothing is certain, the deep relief of your own incredible smallness.

What Calls You

Back then, I wasn't sure what *calling* meant. I thought something mystical—God's hand on my arm, a divine voice speaking my name. Instead, I discovered the colors of cyclamen, how even the meanest weeds burst into bloom.

It works like this—among the books and fires—grace comes disguised as the winter finch, its beak in the seed; the twilight opossum that feeds on scraps—her babies born beneath my neighbor's shed. Every day, I learn what love is: the finches, the opossum, the child with Down Syndrome who asked, *Can I hug you a hundred times?*

Whatever idea I had of myself turns on this: what lives on breath is spirit. I discover the power of simple places—silence—the desire to become nothing.

Beyond Intention

When you appear in your own story exactly as you are—
the blue fire inside the flame, the moon worn smooth—and
you write it down (knowing the perfect fit doesn't exist, a
new easiness that is yours to own). When even the western
light is clear about what you can't understand—how beyond
intention, *this* becomes *that* (precisely because you didn't plan
or prepare for it).

When Everything You've Done and Everything That's Happened to You Is Not What Your Life Is

She's not sure how her life happened or why—the evidence is contradictory (unwise choices, the illnesses, grief—so many portions). A goldfinch sings in the pine, its wing a fragile shadow cast through simple light—the shape of silence.

There are things she's learned to keep from herself—the nightmare she dreamt and re-dreamt until, finally, it meant nothing. The bullet passed through the leaf—the leaf didn't fall.

The stone circle in her yard and the little house are solid in their places—ringed with water and sky. The saplings she planted are firm in the earth. Her dog sleeps beside her (the others dogs' ghosts always close). What else did she want? Things she hoped for already begun—abundant and good.

This

When you walk to the edge of all the light you have . . . you must believe
that one of two things will happen: there will be something solid for you to
stand upon, or, you will be taught how to fly.

— Patrick Overton

The air is luminous, rare—I sit on the old stone bench that
was my mother's and think of her pearls—the fragile string—
how everything rolled into a crack between the wall and
floorboards.

Here there are sparrows at the feeder, crickets in the ivy. Sound
over sound, and bees humming. On the fence beside me, a
spider's web is strung with dust. When a cricket jumps across
my hand, I hold my breath for a second (a way of stopping time
for something perfect).

Everything that needed to be done is done. All *shall* be well,
and all shall be well, and all manner of thing shall be well.*

The branch above me trembles after a bird for which I have
no name; the bird turns and becomes the sky. This is the way
your eyes take in the light, the way you clear the ruins—this
is what saves you.

* Julian of Norwich

✦

THE POEMS in this volume are set in Janson Roman, an elegant old-style typeface based on a design first cut by Tótfalusi Kis in Amsterdam in the Seventeenth Century. The section headings are set in Trajan, Carol Twombly's faithful re-creation into modern typography of the chiseled capitals on ancient Roman monuments.

✦

ACKNOWLEDGMENTS

Grateful acknowledgment is made to the editors and publishers of the following journals, anthologies, and books in which poems from this collection have appeared (some in earlier forms and with earlier titles):

Adanna: How Women Grieve (Adanna Publications, 2012) – "Even Now"

Cape Fear Living – "What to Expect of Heaven" (reprinted by invitation)

Exit 13 – "This," "Without Seeing" (under an earlier title), "as if (this)spring," and "So Much Life"

Ibbetson Street Magazine – "Despite Her Attachment" and "Whatever Meaning"

IthacaLit – "That Should Have Been" and "As Easy As"

Lips – "Why Blueberries?," "No Other World," "What Calls You," and ". . . in this loneliness"

Paterson Literary Review – "Always That Thought," "Something Like Icarus," and "In That Instant" (under an earlier title)

Poetry Pacific – "Even Now," "When Everything You've Done and Everything That's Happened to You Is Not What Your Life Is, " and "Without Seeing" (under an earlier title)

Ragazine – "Twilight and What There Is," "What You Know," and "The Silence After"

Red Wheelbarrow – "Nothing Specific"

Rose Red Review – "Once Upon a . . ."

Shot Glass Journal – "What to Expect of Heaven" and "If It Hadn't Been" *[spaces]* – "This" (reprinted by invitation of the Literary Journal of Trinity Western University)

Stillwater Review – "That Night" (2013 Pushcart Prize Nominee), "No One Said," and "You Reach a Certain Age"

St. Julian Press Website – "This"

Tiferet Journal – "When Everything You've Done and Everything That's Happened to You Is Not What Your Life Is" (in English and in Italian, *"Quando Scopri Che Tutto Ciò Che Hai Fatto e Tutto Ciò Che Ti è Accaduto Non è La Tua Vita,"* translation by Alessandro Pancirolli)

The Poetry Storehouse – "Twilight and What There Is," "What You Know" (with audio by Nic Sebastian), and "The Silence After"

U.S. 1 Worksheets – "And There," "Halloween," and "Something of What"

Wilmington Living – "This" and "When Everything You've Done and Everything That's Happened to You Is Not What Your Life Is" (reprinted by invitation)

An earlier version of "Without Seeing" (under an earlier title) appeared in *What Matters* (Welcome Rain Publishers, 2011).

The epigraph on page vii is by Thomas Merton, from *New Seeds of Contemplation*, copyright ©1961 by The Abbey of Gethsemani, Inc. Reprinted by permission of New Directions Publishing Corp.

Sincerest thanks to my publisher John Weber for all the things that wonderful publishers do, and a big "thank you" to Mara Lurie and Leni Fuhrman.

My most special thanks, always, to Bob Fiorellino and to Alex Pinto for their constancy and love, to Chaucer Kenny for filling the empty spaces with light, and to Charles DeFanti for nearly fifty years of generous friendship and guidance.

NOTES

"Despite Her Attachment" (page 9) is based on Thomas Merton's concluding statement in *New Seeds of Contemplation*—that we are called to deliberately think beyond ourselves, to "forget ourselves on purpose."

". . . in this loneliness" (page 19) is for Joe Weil.

"Even Now" (page 20) is for my father, William Kenny.

The epigraph for "Something Like Icarus" (page 21) is from "Confiteor" (*What Matters*, 2011, Welcome Rain Publishers).

"So Much Life" (page 32) sadly remembers a neighbor who, during a custody dispute in December 2012, locked herself, her three-year-old son, and her Afghan Hound inside a bedroom of their home and set the room on fire.

"Just Perhaps" (page 33) is based on *Ophelia*, a painting by Pre-Raphaelite John Everett Millais and is in memory of Leslie James Price.

"as if (this)spring" (page 37) was sparked, in part, by E. E. Cummings's "Spring is like perhaps a hand."

In "One Day" (page 44), "Shelley's hectic red" is from "Ode to the West Wind" by Percy Bysshe Shelley.

"Because Someone Told Me That Happiness Is an Inside Job" (page 46) is for Alex Pinto.

"No Other World" (page 52) is grateful to Charles Simic's "My Turn to Confess."

The epigraph for "This" (page 60) is from Patrick Overton's poem "Faith" (from patrickoverton.com, credited as © Patrick Overton, The Leaning Tree, 1975, Rebuilding the Front Porch of America, 1997). Source: http://www.patrickoverton.com/poster.html. The quote within the poem's text is, as noted, from Julian of Norwich, a fourteenth-century English mystic. It also appears in T. S. Eliot's "Little Gidding."

About the Author

Adele Kenny's poems, reviews, and articles have been published worldwide, and her poems have appeared in books and anthologies published by Crown, Tuttle, Shambhala, and McGraw-Hill. She is the recipient of various awards, including two poetry fellowships from the NJ State Arts Council, first place Merit Book and Henderson Awards, a Merton Poetry of the Sacred Award, a Writer's Digest Poetry Award, the 2012 International Book Award for Poetry, and the 2014 Distinguished Alumni Award from Kean University. A former creative writing professor in the College of New Rochelle's Graduate School, she is founding director of the Carriage House Poetry Series and poetry editor of *Tiferet Journal*. She has twice been a featured reader at the Geraldine R. Dodge Poetry Festival and has read in the US, England, Ireland, and France.

Website: www.Adelekenny.com
Poetry Blog: www.adelekenny.blogspot.com